33288084923152

D1379869

Ripley's Believe It or Not!

Developed and produced by Ripley Publishing Ltd

This edition published and distributed by:
Mason Crest Publishers Inc.
370 Reed Road, Broomall, Pennsylvania 19008
(866) MCP-BOOK (toll free)
www.masoncrest.com

Copyright © 2004 by Ripley Entertainment Inc. This edition printed in 2009.
All rights reserved. Ripley's, Believe It or Not!, and Ripley's Believe It or Not!
are registered trademarks of Ripley Entertainment Inc.

Ripley's Believe It or Not!
Our Unbelievable Earth
ISBN 978-1-4222-1539-5
Library of Congress Cataloging-in-Publication data is available

Ripley's Believe It or Not!—Complete 16 Title Series
ISBN 978-1-4222-1529-6

No part of this publication may be reproduced in whole or in part, or stored in a retrieval
system, or transmitted in any form or by any means, electronic, mechanical,
photocopying, recording, or otherwise, without written permission from the publishers.
For information regarding permission, write to VP Intellectual Property, Ripley
Entertainment Inc., Suite 188, 7576 Kingspointe Parkway, Orlando, Florida, 32819
email: publishing@ripleys.com

PUBLISHER'S NOTE
While every effort has been made to verify the accuracy of the entries in this book,
the Publishers cannot be held responsible for any errors contained in the work.
They would be glad to receive any information from readers.

WARNING
Some of the stunts and activities in this book are undertaken by experts and should not
be attempted by anyone without adequate training and supervision.

Printed in the United States of America

Ripley's Believe It or Not!

AMAZING EARTH

RIPLEY PUBLISHING

a Jim Pattison Company

Amazing Earth

is a collection of incredible and intriguing facts about a host of stunning natural phenomena. Read about frogs and snakes falling from the sky, a red snowfall in Switzerland, and the day Niagara Falls froze—all in this astonishing book.

Bathers immerse themselves in hot volcanic mud in Colombia...

Babes in the Cosmos

Life appeared on Earth some 3.8 billion years ago, but humans have only been around for about 600,000 years.

If the history of the universe could be compressed into 24 hours, Earth began to be formed out of cosmic dust at around 9:40 a.m. Life appeared on Earth by 4 p.m. The first people walked on the face of our planet at only 11:59 p.m!

Our planet is about a third as old as the universe: Earth is between 4.3 and 4.55 billion years old, and the universe is approximately 11.2 billion years old.

Leveling of Lisbon One of Europe's worst earthquakes was in Lisbon, Portugal, in 1755. The city was wrecked and up to 60,000 people died. The opera singer Antonio Morelli (1739–1814), was buried alive under the rubble of a church destroyed in the quake. His hair had turned white.

High Speed Shock The shock waves forming an earthquake can travel at 5 mi (8 km) a second.

Ripling Rock In Holl Loch cave, Switzerland, two large stalactites hanging on a cave wall resemble flags flying in the wind.

Unshaken The Antarctic has active volcanoes and young mountain ranges, but it is the only part of the Earth that never experiences earthquakes.

Deep Tones A pipe organ was built in the Luray Caverns, in Virginia, using stalactites.

The Cave of the Swallows This deep, vertical cavern is named for the tens of thousands of swallows that live in it. Adventurers reach the floor of the huge cave, which is tall enough to hold the Empire State Building, by rappelling or parachuting—trying not to catch a swallow on the way down.

> **"Gosses Bluff, asteroid... 3,300 ft in diameter"**

Gosses Bluff, a crater in Australia's Northern Territory, seen from space. The asteroid or comet that caused it was probably 0.6 mi (1 km) in diameter and it crashed into Earth about 142 million years ago, creating a ring of hills about 2.8 mi (4.5 km) wide.

Professors Giuseppe Geraci and Bruno D'Argenio from Naples found signs of life snuggled inside meteorites from outer space. Seen here showing their find, they discovered that once the microorganisms were revived they began to move and reproduce rapidly!

Biggest in U.S. A man drilling for water at Manson, Iowa, in 1912 found an unusual rock at the bottom of a well shaft. It was created by the impact of an asteroid 70 million years ago. The huge rock from space, which was 1.5 mi (2.5 km) wide, was the largest known meteorite ever to have hit the U.S. mainland. It made a crater 3 mi (5 km) deep.

Two Miles Down The East Rand Mine, a working gold mine in South Africa, is 11,760 ft (3,585 m) deep.

Blast From Space
On June 30, 1908, reindeer herders in the Tunguska region of Siberia were sent flying into the air by a huge explosion. They had been sleeping in their tents unaware that a meteorite, or a small asteroid, was heading toward them. About 4 mi (6.5 km) up in the atmosphere, the intruder from space exploded. The reindeer herders were thrown into the air and knocked unconscious. One man was killed. The mysterious object in the sky appeared to the men on the ground as if it were a great fireball. On the ground, trees caught fire. After the strange event, dust and smoke were all that remained of 40 sq mi (104 sq km) of forest.

Steady Pounding Around 20 substantial meteorites hit our planet annually. Wethersfield, Connecticut, is the only place to be struck twice by large meteorites—once in April 1971 and again in November 1982.

Well to Hell In a remote region of Russia, near the border with Finland, scientists have dug a hole 8 mi (13 km) deep. Called the Kola Well, it is the deepest hole in the world. Drilling began in 1970 and stopped in 1994. At the bottom of the hole, nicknamed the Well to Hell, scientists found rocks 2.7 billion years old.

The giant rocking stone of Mt. Cimino, Italy, is 28 ft (9 m) long and weighs 385 tons, yet it rocks to and fro on its base without falling off!

Cool Cave Dwellers

The 4,000 residents of Coober Pedy, in the Australian outback, live underground to escape the blistering surface heat.

Above ground it reaches 120°F (49°C), while below ground it is a more comfortable 70°F (21°C). Almost all the population of this outback opal-mining community live below ground, where houses, churches, offices, shops, and hotels have been built. A new five-room house can be constructed with a tunnelling machine for a modest $25,000 (£14,000). The extremely harsh lunar-like landscape of this town also contains a grassless golf course where players carry around a small square of artificial turf from which they tee off!

"Crocodile Harry," a former crocodile hunter, stands in front of the walls of his underground home, which are littered with messages left by tourists who visit this subterranean mining town. Harry's house was featured in the film Mad Max: Beyond Thunderdome *(Aus 1985).*

The minister of the local church stands at the rear of the Coober Pedy underground catacomb church.

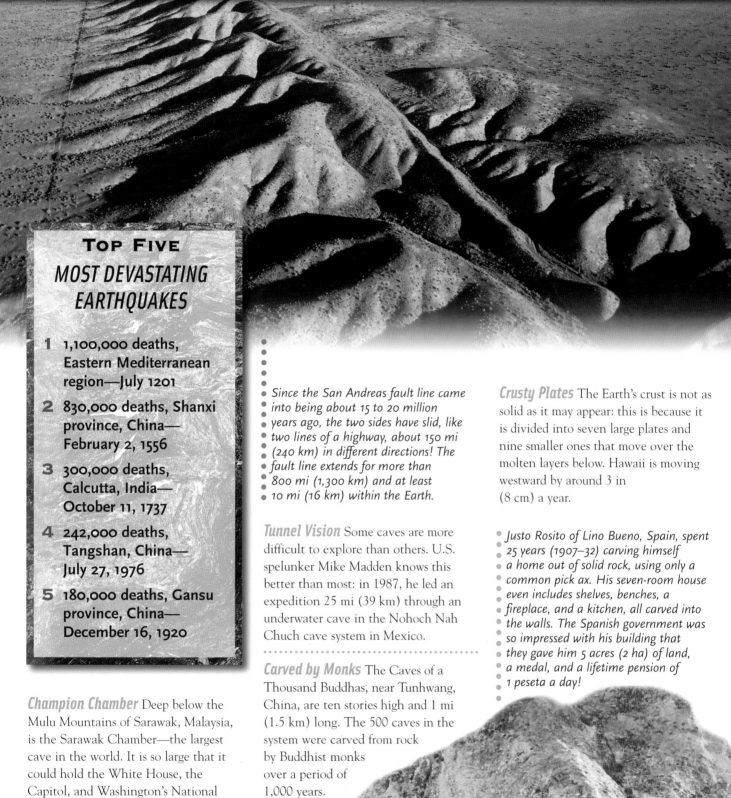

TOP FIVE

MOST DEVASTATING EARTHQUAKES

1 1,100,000 deaths, Eastern Mediterranean region—July 1201

2 830,000 deaths, Shanxi province, China—February 2, 1556

3 300,000 deaths, Calcutta, India—October 11, 1737

4 242,000 deaths, Tangshan, China—July 27, 1976

5 180,000 deaths, Gansu province, China—December 16, 1920

Since the San Andreas fault line came into being about 15 to 20 million years ago, the two sides have slid, like two lines of a highway, about 150 mi (240 km) in different directions! The fault line extends for more than 800 mi (1,300 km) and at least 10 mi (16 km) within the Earth.

Tunnel Vision Some caves are more difficult to explore than others. U.S. spelunker Mike Madden knows this better than most: in 1987, he led an expedition 25 mi (39 km) through an underwater cave in the Nohoch Nah Chuch cave system in Mexico.

Carved by Monks The Caves of a Thousand Buddhas, near Tunhwang, China, are ten stories high and 1 mi (1.5 km) long. The 500 caves in the system were carved from rock by Buddhist monks over a period of 1,000 years.

Crusty Plates The Earth's crust is not as solid as it may appear: this is because it is divided into seven large plates and nine smaller ones that move over the molten layers below. Hawaii is moving westward by around 3 in (8 cm) a year.

Justo Rosito of Lino Bueno, Spain, spent 25 years (1907–32) carving himself a home out of solid rock, using only a common pick ax. His seven-room house even includes shelves, benches, a fireplace, and a kitchen, all carved into the walls. The Spanish government was so impressed with his building that they gave him 5 acres (2 ha) of land, a medal, and a lifetime pension of 1 peseta a day!

Champion Chamber Deep below the Mulu Mountains of Sarawak, Malaysia, is the Sarawak Chamber—the largest cave in the world. It is so large that it could hold the White House, the Capitol, and Washington's National Mall. Every night at dusk three million bats emerge from the mouth of Deer Cave, one of the three other huge caves in the area.

Miles of Darkness The Mammoth Cave system in Kentucky is more than 1,000 mi (1,600 km) long. If the cave tunnels were joined in a straight line, they would stretch from Detroit to New York City.

Molten Gold
When Mount Erebus, Antarctica, erupts, it throws out pieces of pure gold in its volcanic lava.

At approximately 4 a.m. on August 24, CE 79 Mount Vesuvius erupted and killed the inhabitants of Pompeii, burying them under a fine ash that petrified and solidified over time. The flesh and organs decomposed leaving behind the shape of those that had died.

Josefsberg, a village in South Tyrol, Italy, is in perpetual shadow for 91 days of the year. The mountains cut off the Sun from November 3 until February 2.

Overnight Success
Vulcan Island, in Rabaul Harbor, Papua New Guinea, rose from the ocean floor in a single night in 1870. Within a few years, the volcano had grown to become a 600 ft (180 m) peak. Cooled lava eventually joined Vulcan to the mainland.

Bridge Builder
Mount Sakurajima in Japan was an island until 1914, when it erupted so violently that its lava filled a strait 1,000 ft (300 m) wide and 300 ft (90 m) deep, making the island part of the mainland.

Surprise Crop
Mexican farmer Dominic Pulido witnessed the birth of a volcano in 1943. Working in his fields, he saw a hole open in the ground, from which smoke and dust emerged as well as sulphurous materials. Slowly, a tiny volcanic cone formed. Now called Paricutin, the volcano had reached a height of 1,391 ft (424 m) by the time it became dormant in 1952. Robert Ripley tried to buy this volcano!

Lassen Volcanic National Park, northern California, attracts many tourists who want to stand on "California's Hot Rock." The rock remained hot for three weeks after being blown 3 mi (5 km) from the crater of Mt. Lassen when it erupted in 1915.

Explosive Exit
Krakatoa, a volcano in Indonesia, completely disappeared on August 26, 1883. The island volcano was ripped apart by an eruption and the whole island was destroyed. The explosion was heard over 10 percent of the globe. Near the volcano, the Sun was blocked out, and dust was still falling 10 days later.

People frequently immerse themselves in the supposedly therapeutic hot mud that fills the crater within Totumo volcano, in Colombia.

"Totumo volcano in Colombia spurts mud 50 ft in the air"

Deep Sea Fire A volcano 39,000 ft (12,000 m) below the waters of the Bismarck Sea, off Papua New Guinea, emits tiny amounts of molten silver and gold when it erupts.

Sole Survivor Only one person escaped the eruption of Mont Pelée, on the Caribbean island of Martinique, in 1902. Everyone in the town of St. Pierre, at the foot of the volcano, perished, except a prisoner being held in a thick-walled cell.

Afterglow After the eruption of Mont Pelée, the tower of lava it threw up glowed so much that it lit up the night sky above for months.

Now You See It, Now You Don't Giulia Ferdinanda, a tiny volcanic island off the coast of Sicily, Italy, regularly emerges from, and disappears under, the waves of the Mediterranean Sea.

Growing in Peak Season Showa Shinzan in Japan is the fastest-growing young volcano. The cone appeared on December 28, 1943 and erupted the following year, by which time it had reached a height of 656 ft (200 m). It has now reached a height of 2,400 ft (732 m)—and is still growing!

Driven Inland The eruption of Krakatoa unleashed a tidal wave that washed the Dutch ship *Berouw* some 2 mi (3 km) up onto the shore.

TOP FIVE
DEVASTATING VOLCANIC ERUPTIONS

1 **Unnamed volcano— New Zealand—*c.* CE 130.** Huge crater now filled by Lake Taupo, created by massive explosion that threw out 30 million tons of ash

2 **Santorini (Thera)— Greece, *c.* 1550 BCE.** Volcanic explosion caused a tidal wave that may have wiped out the ancient Minoan civilization in Crete

3 **Krakatoa—Indonesia, 1883.** The volcanic eruption threw material 34 mi (55 km) in the air

4 **Tambora—Indonesia, 1815.** Top of the volcanic cone was lowered by about 4,000 ft (1,219 m) in seconds by the force of the eruption

5 **Vesuvius—Italy, CE 79.** The Roman towns of Pompeii, Herculaneum, and Stabiae were buried under ash clouds of gas

Erik Weihenmayer, seen here about to cross a ravine, became the first blind person to climb to the summit of Mount Everest in 2001. He has also conquered the seven tallest summits of the world's seven continents as well as the Polar Circus, a 3,000 ft (900 m) ice waterfall in Alberta.

Mounting Everest The height of Mount Everest increased by 6 ft (2 m) in 1999. The official height was changed as a result of using the satellite-based technology of the Global Positioning System (GPS).

Shell Shock Fossils of creatures that once lived in the sea have been found near the summit of Everest.

Fast Climb Sherpa Lhakpa Gelu conquered Everest in record time— 10 hours 56 minutes in May 2003.

Summit to Brag About Earth is not a perfect ball shape, so the summit of the Andean peak Chimorazo—20,561 ft (6,267 m) high—is farther from the Earth's center than the summit of the highest peak—Mount Everest 29,035 ft (8,850 m) high.

Highly Mistaken Pico de Teide, in the Canary Islands, was once thought to be the world's highest mountain, but poor measurement had overestimated its height by several thousand feet.

HIGH LIFE

- Sherpa Apa has climbed Mt. Everest 13 times!
- American Gary Guller was the first one-armed person to climb Mt. Everest in 2003
- In 2001 Marco Siffredi descended from the summit of Mt. Everest on his snowboard
- Davo Karnicar in 2000 came down Mt. Everest on skis
- The only person to have slept on the summit of Mt. Everest was Sherpa Babu, who spent over 21 hours there in 1999

Running on Thin Air Italian mountaineer Rheinhold Meissner was the first person to climb the world's 14 highest mountains—all the peaks above 26,250 ft (8,000 m)—without using oxygen.

At the age of 70 years, 222 days Japanese professional skier Yuichiro Miura (left) and his son display their flag at the summit of Everest. He broke the record for the oldest person to climb the peak in May 2002.

Over 2,200 climbers have reached the top of Mount Everest and at least 170 have died in the attempt.

"Over 2,200 have reached the top of Everest"

Talking Mountain The roaring mountain of Fallon, Nevada, is composed of sharp, fine, white sand. At times the sound of it rumbling and roaring can be heard for miles.

Climb on a Bus The highest point of the world's lowest-lying nation—the Maldives—is about the same height as a school bus.

Equatorial Snow Mount Kenya is situated on the Equator in tropical Africa, but despite this it is always covered with snow.

Sea for Miles Vatnajökull, in Iceland, can be seen from the Faroe Islands, 340 mi (547 km) away—the world's longest view between mountains.

Vanishing Peak In 1991, the top 33 ft (10 m) of New Zealand's Mount Cook, (the country's highest mountain) fell off in an avalanche. The peak now measures 12,316 ft (3,754 m).

Ocean Views Standing atop Costa Rica's Mount Izaru, which rises to 11,200 ft (3,414 m), a person can see both the Pacific and Atlantic oceans.

Undersea Mountains The world's longest mountain chain is under the sea. The Mid-Ocean Ridge snakes beneath the waters of the Pacific, Arctic, Atlantic, and Indian oceans for about 52,080 mi (83,812 km). This submarine mountain chain is almost 11 times longer than the Andes, the longest range of mountains on land.

Silbury Hill in Wiltshire, England, is very strange. It is a mound containing 1,250,000 tons of earth built by prehistoric man for no apparent reason!

Tabletops The flat mountain tablelands of Venezuela—called tepuis—are among the most unusual mountains in the world. The largest tepui is called Roraima, a 44 sq mi (113 sq km) tableland that rises in sheer cliffs some 9,200 ft (2,804 m) high. On this isolated tableland, all of the plant species are native, and are not found anywhere else in the world.

Lightning Strikes Seven Times!

Roy Sullivan, a park ranger in Yosemite National Park, California, survived seven lightning strikes during his life. The first strike in 1969 singed his eyebrows.

The next year he suffered burns to his left shoulder. Three more strikes followed in 1972 and 1973. The first set light to his hair—he extinguished the flames by throwing a bucket of water over his head. Just as his hair had grown back, another bolt ripped through his hat and struck his head, setting his hair on fire again. The third bolt caused an injury to his ankle. Four years later, lightning burned his chest and stomach. Finally, he survived a lightning strike that brought power lines crashing into the cabin where he was living.

BOLTS FROM THE BLUE

- A lightning bolt, on average, is 2 mi (3 km) long and 3 in (8 cm) wide
- 84 percent of people struck by lightning are male
- The temperature of a lightning bolt can reach 540,000°F (300,000°C)—about six times hotter than the surface of the Sun
- At any given moment, there are about 1800 thunderstorms raging around the world, generating 50 to 100 sky-to-ground lightning strikes each minute
- Lightning can travel through the air at about 90,000 mi (145,000 km) a second—nearly half the speed of light

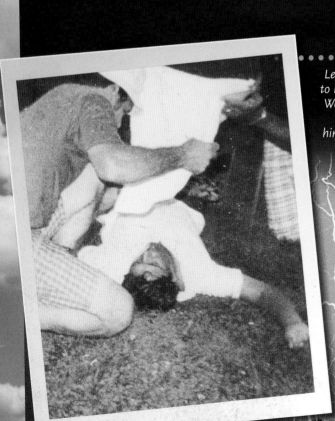

Lee Trevino was one of four golfers to be struck by lightning during the Western Open tournament held in Chicago in 1975. The bolt threw him 18 in (46 cm) into the air and knocked him unconscious.

One Hot Town Residents of Bremanger on the Norwegian coast blame a nearby power line for attracting lightning bolts that have struck all 11 houses in the village at least once in the last 35 years. One house, belonging to Klara and Kare Svarstad, was struck by lightning four times in 1999.

JUMPING THE GUN
In June 1987, lightning triggered the launch mechanisms of three rockets at NASA's Wallops Island, Virginia, launchpad. Ironically, the rockets were fitted with instruments designed to investigate lightning. "We were hoping for lightning. We just had it a little closer than we would like," said Warren Gurkin, head of NASA's sounding rocket projects branch.

Homes Blown In May 1951, lightning set fire to two houses in Marianna, Florida—one belonging to C.N. Horne of North Green Street, and the other to S. H. Horne of South Green Street.

Mass Barbeque On June 22, 1918, 504 sheep were killed by a single lightning strike in the Wasatch National Forest, Utah.

Miracle Flash Nine years after being blinded in an accident, Edwin Robinson of Falmouth, Maine, recovered his sight after being struck by lightning on June 4, 1980.

Bolt Triggers Disaster During a thunderstorm on November 2, 1994 a bolt of lightning derailed a train carrying fuel oil through the southern Egyptian town of Drunka. The lightning ignited the oil, which in turn set fire to an oil depot close to the crash site. The blazing oil was carried through the town by the torrential rainwater, killing an estimated 500 people.

Heavenly Message In July 1984 three days after a bishop with controversial views was consecrated in York Minster, a thunderbolt struck the cathedral, causing more than $ 3.5 million (£2 million) damage.

Strokes of Luck If you have been struck by lightning and survived, you are eligible for membership of the Lightning Strike Survivors club with its motto "Join us if it strikes you."

High Toll A deadly lightning bolt struck a Boeing 707 in 1963, causing the plane to crash, killing 81 people.

Team Loss All 11 members of a soccer team were killed by lightning, during a match in the Democratic Republic of the Congo on October 25, 1998. The other team was untouched.

Winning Charge In 1910, Ray Caldwell, a baseball pitcher for the Cleveland Indians, was struck by lightning and knocked out, but went on to finish and win the game.

Scorched Earth In the Xinjian Uygur autonomous region of China, there is a 60-mi (100-km) long area where freak lightning storms regularly cause trees to burst into flames.

The Empire State Building in New York—and the Eiffel Tower in Paris—are struck by lightning an average of 20 to 30 times a year because lightning usually seeks out the highest object

Thomas the Tank Engine and his Friends were frozen in ice at the annual Japanese snow and ice sculpture festival in Sapporo, Japan. More than 3,000 people are needed to build the largest sculptures.

Holy Sign In August 2000, in Ontario, Canada, a lightning bolt ripped through a tree and set an empty three-bedroom cottage ablaze. In the ashes all that was left was a plaque of the Virgin Mary.

Frozen Funerals In the Russian city of Yakutsk, which lies deep in eastern Siberia, the ground is frozen so hard that graves can only be dug from March through September during the thaw. The citizens of Yakutsk must postpone the burial part of all funerals until summer.

COLORED SNOW
Red snow fell on part of the Swiss Alps on October 1775, and chocolate-colored snow fell on Mount Hotham, in Victoria, Australia, in July 1935. The red snowflakes were colored by sand dust blown north from the Sahara, while the chocolate snow held dust from Victoria's dry Mallée district.

Whits Sands On January 6, 1913, 4 in (10 cm) of snow fell on Jabal Gargaf, Libya, in the Sahara Desert.

High Fall The deepest snow after one snowfall was appropriately at Mount Shasta Ski Bowl, California, from February 13 through February 19, 1959. This prolonged white-out resulted in 189 in (4.8 m) of snow.

Ski Polars Russian Dmitry Shparo and six members of his team, were the first to ski to the North Pole. Their 900 mi (1,448 km) journey took 77 days.

Cloaked in White The deepest snowfall ever recorded was 38 ft (11.5 m). This astonishing blanket of snow piled up during a single blizzard on March 11, 1911 in Tamarac, California.

Tusk, Tusk! In 1997, six elephants were killed by a single lightning bolt in Kruger National Park, South Africa.

Snowmobile Sojourn U.S. brothers Andre, Carl, and Denis Boucher—along with John Outzen in 1992—crossed the snow and ice of the North America polar cap, from the Pacific to the Atlantic, on snowmobiles. They took 56 days to cover the 10,250 mi (16,495 km) from Alaska to Nova Scotia.

In 1997, Norwegian explorer Boerge Ousland traveled solo across Antarctica in 64 days. He became the first person to journey unaided across the snowy southern continent.

Hailstones the size of tennis balls were collected by storm chasers after a hailstorm near Sitka, Kansas in 1999.

SNOW IN THE DESERT
The Gulf emirate of Dubai will have snow starting in 2006. A $277 (£153) million "ski dome" is being constructed in the desert to bring winter sports to the Arabian peninsula. The dome, which will be open to public skiing, will include a revolving ski slope through an artificial mountain.

Ice Blanket In August 1980, residents of Orient, Nebraska, were startled to see white drifts of hail blanketing their neighborhood. The hail had covered the ground to a depth of 6 ft 6 in (2 m).

Slow Thaw The amount of hail that fell on Adair and Union Counties, Texas, in August 1890, was so heavy that some stayed on the ground for six months.

Heavy! Hailstones that weighed more than 2 lb 3 oz (1 kg) fell on Gopalganj in Bangladesh in 1986.

Fatal Fall On July 19, 2002, hailstones the size of hen's eggs fell in Henan province, China. There were 25 fatalities, many people were hospitalized with head wounds, buildings were destroyed, and the windows of vehicles were smashed.

Handful of Hail A giant hailstone was found in Coffeyville, Kansas, on September 3, 1970. When scientist Nancy Knight held the hailstone in her hand, it was larger than her palm.

TOP FIVE
STRANGEST RAINS
We're not serious when we say it's raining cats and dogs, but history has recorded some unusual precipitation.

1 **Dead mice**—Bergen, Norway, 1578

2 **Live toads**—Lalain, France, 1794

3 **Live snakes**—Memphis, Tennessee, 1877

4 **Live mussels**—Paderborn, Germany, 1892

5 **Live maggots**—Acapulco, Mexico, 1968

"Hailstones the size of hen's eggs killed 25 people in China"

Hail Horror The deadliest hailstorm on record killed 246 people and more than 1,600 farm animals in Moradabad, India, on April 30, 1888.

Crossroads near Hitzacker in Germany, in 2002 were cut off by rising water levels, caused by the surging River Elbe overflowing its banks.

This mule, belonging to dairy farmer W.T. Perry of Jefferson County, Kentucky, climbed into a tree to escape a flood in January 1937.

DON'T LOOK UP!

Frogs and toads showered down on the residents of Leicester, Massachusetts, on September 7, 1954. Tiny frogs fell from the sky in many parts of Gloucestershire, England, in October 1987; a shower of frogs occurred during a storm at Brignoles, France, on September 23, 1973, and Sylvia Mowday and her daughter were showered with tiny frogs in Birmingham, England, on June 12, 1954.

Rainfree No rain has fallen on parts of the Atacama Desert in northern Chile in recorded history.

Seeing Red On June 30, 1968, it rained blood in Britain. Upon closer examination it was found that the rain had been stained by red sand—which had come from the Sahara Desert, some 2,000 mi (3,200 km) away!

Wettest Places Every year, 467 in (12 m) of rain falls on Mawayram, India. The wettest place in the U.S. is Mount Waialeale, Hawaii, which gets 460 in (11.7 m) of rain a year.

Heaviest Rain In 1952, the heaviest single rainfall ever, dropped more than 7,500 tons of water on one acre (0.4 ha) of land on the Indian Ocean island of Réunion.

Greatest Gust The strongest wind ever recorded in the U. S.—and the highest wind speed at ground level ever recorded on Earth—was a gust of 231 mph (372 km/h) on Mount Washington, New Hampshire, on April 12, 1934.

Hold On! The world's windiest place is Commonwealth Bay, Antarctica, where gales regularly reach as much as 200 mph (322 km/h).

The end of this house was carried away by a tornado, but the dishes in the pantry remained intact where they were!

Heavy Oil Deposit
A tornado that struck Bakersfield, California, in 1990 moved two 90-ton oil drums 3 mi (4.8 km), depositing them 600 ft (183 m) up the side of a mountain.

Fast Track
A tornado that swept through Wichita Falls, Texas, on April 2, 1958, traveled at a speed of 280 mph (451 km/h).

Tornado Festival
Between April 3 and 4, 1974, the U.S. experienced 148 tornadoes.

Hot Shade
The highest temperature ever recorded was 136°F (58°C) in the shade at Al'Aziziyah, in Libya, on September 13, 1922.

Cold Out There!
The coldest temperature ever recorded on Earth was –128.6°F (–89°C) at Vostok base, Antarctica, on July 21, 1983.

On average, there are 140 tornadoes annually in the U.S.

Sunglass Cities
Sun-worshipers should head for either Yuma, Arizona, which has the highest annual average days of sunshine in the world, or St. Petersburg, Florida, where the Sun shone for 768 consecutive days from February 1967 through March 1969.

Flying Cow
In 1878, a tornado in Iowa carried a cow about 10 mi (16 km) through the air.

Off the Rails
On May 29, 1934, a tornado at Moorhead, Minnesota, lifted and carried an eight-car passenger train 80 ft (24 m) from the railroad tracks.

Flying Hound
In 1994, at Le Mars, Iowa, a tornado picked up a dog and its doghouse, depositing them both unharmed several blocks away.

A Ball at the Falls

After Lussier's successful descent of the falls, he sold off pieces of his rubber ball to tourists. When he sold out he reportedly began selling pieces of rubber that he had bought from a nearby tire store!

Jean Lussier, a 36-year-old from Massachusetts, made history by going over Niagara Falls in an inflatable rubber ball, rather than a wooden barrel or steel drum. He lived to tell the tale.

Lussier put his $1,500 (£800) life savings into building the 6-ft (1.8-m) diameter rubber ball, lined with 32 inner tubes to protect against shock, and an empty interior with an air cushion for protection. The ball had 150 lb (68 kg) of hard rubber ballast placed at the bottom to keep it stable, and contained enough oxygen to keep Lussier alive for 40 hours in case he was trapped under the water. On July 4, 1928, he rowed his ball out into the middle of the river, 2 mi (3 km) upstream of Horseshoe Falls. Cut free, the ballast immediately ripped from the bottom of the ball, before Lussier went over the edge at 3.35 p.m. Three of the inner tubes burst in the fall and the frame was badly damaged. However, at 4.23 p.m. the rubber ball and Lussier were picked up by the *Maid of the Mist*, a sight-seeing tourist boat. Lussier survived and only suffered minor bruising!

William Red Hill Sr. in his steel barrel in 1930 before his successful navigation of the lower rapids and whirlpool at Niagara Falls. In 1951, his son, Red Hill Jr. repeated his father's stunt in a barrel made of rubber tubes—but died in the attempt.

DAREDEVILS

In October 1829, Sam Patch became the first person to leap over Niagara Falls. He jumped twice, with no protection. "No one ought ever do that again," said Annie Taylor, the first person and only woman to go over the falls, after she successfully plunged over Niagara Falls in a barrel in October 1901 at the age of 63. In July 1920, Englishman Charles Stevens went over the edge in a barrel with an anvil tied to his feet. All that was found of him was an arm attached to the barrel. Robert Overacker fell to his death in 1995 having attempted the jump on a jet ski and rocket backpack.

Deluge The biggest flood ever occurred about 7,500 years ago when water poured over a narrow lowland to the east of the Mediterranean, creating the Black Sea. This torrent drowned towns, villages, and farms, and may have been the flood in the Bible story of Noah.

Washed Away In the 1540s, the city of Ciudad Vieja in Guatemala was destroyed when a huge wave of water was released from beneath Mount Agua during an earthquake.

Call of the Falls In 1855, explorer David Livingstone became the first non-African to see the falls he named the Victoria Falls. However, he actually heard the roar of the falls when he was still 20 mi (32 km) away. The local name for the waterfall, Mosi-oa-tunya ("the waters that thunder"), could not be more appropriate.

When floods swept away crops and homes in Mozambique in 2000, Sophia Pedro was forced to take refuge from the rising waters in a tree. High in its branches, she gave birth to a baby, Rositha. An hour later, soldier Stewart Back was lowered from a South African military helicopter to rescue mother and baby.

Frozen Stiff On March 29, 1849 during extremely cold weather, an ice jam temporarily stopped the massive flow of water over Niagara Falls.

Falls Facts An amazing 370,000 tons of water pass over Niagara Falls every moment, but even at this rate, it would take more than 2 million years for all the water on Earth to flow over Niagara. The greatest waterfalls on Earth by volume, however, are the Buyoma Falls on the Congo River. Three times as much water plunges over Buyoma than the cascade over Niagara.

Highest The steepest waterfall is Angel Falls on the Carrao River in Venezuela. The falls drop a total of 3,212 ft (979 m), with the highest individual fall being 2,648 ft (807 m).

The Leukbach, a tributary of the Saar River in Germany, plunges over a fall as it races through a narrow street in Saarburg.

Fall Moon Cumberland Falls, Kentucky, is one of only two waterfalls on Earth that form a moonbow—a feature resembling a rainbow but seen by the light of the moon reflected on water. During a full moon, the colored moonbow is seen in the waters of the 150-ft (46-m) wide waterfall.

The Tonle Sap River, Cambodia, flows south in January, north from February to June, then changes back to south again for the rest of the year.

Ice Cliff A frozen waterfall has been discovered on the slopes of Mount Beardmore. More than 10,000 ft (3,084 m) of vertical ice now marks the former waterfall that was once 60 times the height of 160 ft (50 m) of Niagara Falls.

Rise and Fall Lake Wakatipu in New Zealand changes its level at least 320 times every day! The 52-mi (84-km) river rises and falls 3 in (7 cm) every five minutes.

Two-way Current The Baleswar River in India flows both north and south in the rainy season. It flows southward at the surface while its lower currents race in the opposite direction.

Deepest Valley Carved by a tumbling torrent, Tibet's Yarlung Zangbo is the deepest valley on Earth: its depth is equivalent to 22 times the height of the Statue of Liberty.

Tide Rules River water does not always flow to the sea: In the lowest section of the river the tide reverses the flow. The tidal wave that sweeps upstream on the Qiantong Jiang river in China is 25 ft (8 m) high.

Shortest River The world's shortest river, Montana's North Fork Roe River, is only 58 ft (17.7 m) long.

Hidden Falls Trümmelbach Cascade, a waterfall in Switzerland, is invisible for much of its height because it is inside the core of Mt. Jungfrau.

John-Paul Eatock and his Jack Russell, Part-Ex, brave swirling waters while white water swimming. This action dog also takes part in windsurfing, kayaking, rock jumping, and parachute jumping!

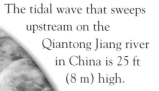

For half the year the water at The Trick Falls at Glacier National Park, Montana goes over the high falls, and for the other half it falls under the high falls! The reason for this is that underneath the rock precipice is a subterranean outlet for the waters of the river above. During the dry season this underground passage is large enough to hold the entire flow of the river and water goes under the falls (see bottom). During the wet season the falls increase so that the underground river is entirely hidden and the water cascades over the top falls (see top).

DISAPPEARING LAKE

Africa's Lake Chad is now only 500 sq mi (1,350 sq km) in area. Prolonged drought since the 1960s has dramatically reduced its extent from a once staggering 10,000 sq mi (26,000 sq km) in the wetter months. But evidence from abandoned shorelines, that has recently been discovered, shows that the lake was once more than 12 times as large as it is today.

Deep Freeze The ground is frozen solid to a depth of 4,500 ft (1,400 m) beneath parts of Siberia—that's over three times the height of New York's Empire State Building!

Great Depression The basin that contains the Caspian Sea is so large that it could contain Missouri, Iowa, Illinois, New Hampshire, and Vermont. The Caspian lowland is the world's largest depression.

Lifeless Arab Plain Cover all of Texas with sand and you would have a desert the same size as Arabia's Empty Quarter (the Rub al-Khali), which is the world's largest expanse of sand. The Empty Quarter has no water and almost no life.

Dune of Oz The longest sand dunes are in Australia's Simpson Desert. They stretch in parallel lines a distance equal to from Washington D.C. to Philadelphia.

Dank Desert Around 90 percent of the sand in the Kara Kum Desert in Central Asia is black.

Color Map Trackers can find their way around the Namib Desert, along the coast of Namibia, southern Africa, by the color of the sand. The farther inland the sand, the older it is and the longer it has been baked rusty red in the Sun.

Singing Sands Winds blowing over the sand dunes in the Gobi Desert in Mongolia, cause a constant sound that varies from drum roll sounds to a deep chant.

A Desert is Born The world's newest desert appeared in 2001. The Hamoun, on the borders of Iran and Afghanistan, is normally a great wetland that varies in size between 400 and 800 sq mi (1,035 to 2,070 sq km). However, unreliable rainfall in the distant mountains that feed the rivers flowing toward the Hamoun, periodically turns the marsh and lake into a desert. From 1999 through 2001, these mountains experienced an extended period of drought. As a result, the Hamoun is now a salt desert. When the rivers flow again, it will fill with water.

TOP FIVE
DESERT EXPANSES

1 Sahara, North Africa— 3,250,000 sq mi (8,416,850 sq km)

2 Australian Desert, central Australia— 600,000 sq mi (1,553,880 sq km)

3 Arabian Desert, Oman/ Saudi— 500,000 sq mi (1,294,900 sq km)

4 Gobi Desert, Mongolia/China— 400,000 sq mi (1,035,920 sq km)

5 Kalahari Desert, Botswana— 200,000 sq mi (517,960 sq km)

The Aral Sea formerly was the world's fourth largest lake covering 26,250 sq mi (68,000 sq km), equal to the area of southern California. Today, it has decreased by 75 percent, the equivalent of draining Lake Ontario and Lake Erie. The sea level has fallen by 50 ft (16 m) leaving abandoned ships sitting on the sand.

Brutal, Dry, Run to a Hot Finish

The annual 105-mi (160-km) nonstop Desert Cup race across the arid desert of Jordan/Arabia requires the participants to carry their own equipment and supplies—apart from drinking water.

Leaving Petra at the start of their journey, competitors face two days of non-stop running across bleak, barren, desert terrain, stopping only briefly for a rest.

The maximum time allowed to complete the non-stop Desert Cup race is only 60 hours. Competitors race 25 mi (40 km) through mountains, then 35 mi (56 km) running over desert stones, and finally 45 mi (72 km) across sand. The frontrunners in the competition cross the Wadi Rum Desert at night avoiding the intense heat, while those that follow have to run in sweltering 110°F (43°C) heat. The rules state that no runner is allowed to help any other if they get into trouble.

SAND BOWL
The semidesert north and east of Lake Chad in central Africa is the single most important source of dust in Earth's atmosphere. Dust is lifted off the desert's arid, dry surface by winter winds and dispersed through the planet's atmosphere.

Made in the Shade Humans have made 75 percent of the oases in the Sahara Desert. These artificial oases are irrigated valleys in which palm trees have been planted to provide shade from the Sun.

Dead Flat Australia's Nullabor Plain, a featureless, treeless expanse, is so flat that the railroad that crosses the plain runs completely straight for 300 mi (483 km).

Our Own Oasis The largest oasis in the Universe is 7,900 mi (12,713 km) in diameter. Planet Earth is the only known world where plants grow, water flows, and animals live.

Ice Trench The deepest point on land is the Bentley Trench, which lies under the ice of Antarctica. This depression is more than 8,320 ft (2,536 m) below sea level.

Lowland The deepest exposed depression on Earth surrounds the Dead Sea, between Israel and Jordan. The lakeshore is 1,310 ft (399 m) below sea level.

Over a period of 40 years the wind eroded the ground away leaving this pine tree stump in Tuscola County, Michigan, standing 6 ft (2 m) above the ground.

Dry Rot Over time, the advance of the Sahara Desert toward the Mediterranean Sea has buried some 600 Roman cities.

Wide Sahara The Sahara Desert is as large in area as the U.S.A.

A competitor in the 2003 Dakar Rally takes time out to do his ironing—on the roof of his car!

Great Grove! The largest palm grove oasis in the world, at Palm Canyon, California, stretches a distance of 15 mi (38 km) end to end.

Ships in the Sand Seals live in a desert where shipwrecks can be found. The Skeleton Coast of Namibia is a desert landscape where soaring dunes rise from beaches that are home to seal colonies and are littered with remains of craft that have floundered on the treacherous shore.

Hot Airmail The longest regular weekly mail delivery trip into a desert is a 1,625-mi (2,615-km) airplane mail run that sets off from Port Augusta, South Australia, every Saturday for Boulia in the hot dry interior.

Buried in Time Desert sands completely buried the city of Ubar, in Oman. This city was a flourishing trading center 1,700 years ago but it disappeared under the sands and was only rediscovered in 1974.

Last March An entire army disappeared in the desert without a trace. Sent by the Persian king Cambyses in 525 BC to reconquer ancient Egypt, the army was journeying to Siwa Oasis to destroy the temple of the god Amun. The oracle of the temple prophesized that the army would be defeated. It vanished in the Western Desert.

Just outside Tucson, Arizona, in the Sonora Desert, lies an airplane graveyard. Nearly 4,400 decommissioned airplanes and helicopters lie abandoned over 2,600 acres (1,050 ha) of land. The desert's climate stops the planes from deteriorating or corroding too quickly, and millions of dollars of spare parts are regularly salvaged from the planes. The FBI uses the site for rehearsing airplane hostage rescues.

"Entire army vanished in the desert without a trace"

This tree growing in the middle of U.S. highway 60 near Fairland, Oklahoma, can never be cut down. The deed for the land for the highway was given to the state on the proviso that the tree never be disturbed. The elm was planted by a small boy in honor of his deceased father.

A mirage seen in the sky over Ashland, Ohio, on March 12, 1890, appeared to be a reflection of another town some 30 mi (50 km) away.

From Green to Grit Twenty thousand years ago, the Sahara Desert was actually covered in grasslands, rivers, lakes, and forests, when cool winds from Europe carried moisture to northern Africa.

O.00662

A Gem for the Gulf

The man-made island of Palm Jumeirah, in the Persian Gulf, is the first man-made object to be visible from miles up in the air built since the Great Wall of China.

The enormous artificial island will form part of an enormous complex of islands and causeways, covering more than 3 sq mi (8 sq km) and measuring 4 mi (6.5 km) in length. The island is part of a structure shaped like a palm tree, with a trunk nearly 1 mi (1.5 km) wide and 17 great leafy "fronds." Millionaires and celebrities have bought properties on this luxurious beach resort with its 35 mi (56 km) of artificial beaches, 50 luxury hotels, 4,500 apartments and villas, shopping complexes, cinemas, and marine park.

This satellite image shows the giant palm-tree-shaped island of Jumeirah, off the coast of Dubai, jutting 3 mi (5 km) out into the blue sea.

TOP FIVE
SHORT COASTLINES

Some coutries have unbelievably short coastlines

1 **Monaco**—3 mi (5 km)

2 **Nauru**—12 mi (19 km)

3 **Bosnia-Herzegovina**—13 mi (21 km)

4 **Jordan**—16 mi (26 km)

5 **Slovenia**—19 mi (31 km)

Delta Nation The largest delta in the world is a country—most of Bangladesh, which comprises some 55,600 sq mi (143,993 sq km). It is formed by the combined deltas of the Ganges and Brahmaputra rivers.

Ultrawave! The tallest wave ever to hit the shore was a monster of 1,720 ft (524 m) that battered Lituya Bay, Alaska, in July 1958.

Water Births The world's newest island was a surprise—and so is its name. Surprise Rock Island (Pulau Batu Hairan) off the state of Sabah, Malaysia, rose from the ocean floor in 1988. Several other tiny volcanic islets have appeared from the sea since then but, unlike Surprise Rock Island, they have either sunk back into the ocean or been washed away.

Stranded The longest involuntary stay on an island was that by the crew of the ship *Invercauld*, which was wrecked on sub-Antarctic Auckland Island in May 1864. Only three of the 19 crew were rescued alive 375 days later.

Largest Atoll Kwaljein, in the Pacific island nation of the Marshall Islands, is the world's largest atoll. The thin island bends round to enclose an area the size of Rhode Island.

Island Neighbors The island of Little Diomede, part of the U.S., sits in the Bering Strait between Siberia and Alaska. Two mi (3 km) west of Little Diomede is the island of Big Diomede, part of the former Soviet Union. The position of these two islands means that the former Soviet Union and the U.S. are only a couple of miles apart.

All at Sea The uninhabited bleak and icy island of Bouvet in the Southern Ocean is 1,050 mi (1,690 km) from the nearest land, about the same distance as from Omaha, Nebraska, to Salt Lake City, Utah.

Building Stones At Kotor in Montenegro, locals threw stones at Chisel Rock over a period of 150 years. Eventually, the small rock emerging from the waves was transformed into a more substantial islet, large enough for a church to be constructed on it.

Floridian Iceberg The farthest south an Arctic iceberg has been seen in the Atlantic Ocean was at latitude 28°22'—slightly farther south than Daytona Beach, Florida.

Divers in Egypt in 2001 made an unbelieveable discovery beneath the waves. A statue of the ancient Egyptian god, Hapi, was found at the sunken site of Heracleon.

A sheer rock pinnacle called Ball's Pyramid that rises 1,843 ft (562 m) out of the sea near Lord Howe Island, Australia is 2.5 times the height of the towers of San Francisco's Golden Gate Bridge.

This amazing Olympic torch enables a flame to exist even when submerged in water! It was carried by Wendy Craig Duncan during the preparation for the 2000 Sydney Olympic Games.

Kingdom on Stilts

Roy Bates claims that the "island-fort" he owns, which measures 430 x 120 ft (131 x 37 m), is the smallest state in the world. Eight miles off the eastern coast of England, the fort, a former World War II British Royal Navy fort, named Roughs Tower, stands on stilts above the North Sea.

SHIPWRECK ISLAND

In the Moroni River between Suriname and French Guiana, a wrecked ship has given birth to an island. The vessel slowed the water flow, allowing mud to be deposited. The ship filled with mud, and seeds carried by the water became lodged and germinated. Over a period of 36 years, the shipwreck was transformed into a tiny (nameless) island, sprouting trees.

In 1966, Bates and his wife Joan, declared the fort to be the kingdom of Sealand and themselves to be king and queen, despite never receiving official recognition of such. "King Roy" over time developed national treasures, such as the flag of the Principality of Sealand, a national anthem, gold and silver coins launched as Sealand dollars, stamps, and passports.

Alaska has a coastline that is larger than all the other coastal states in the U.S. combined.

Michael Bates is King Roy's heir apparent to Sealand (seen in the background), the fort they claim to be the smallest state in the world.

Surfing the River

An amazing natural tidal wave races each year up the River Severn in England.

This phenomenon travels up the Severn estuary, tumbling its way for a distance of 25 mi (40 km). The tidal wave, known as a bore, occurs when the volume of water entering the Bristol Channel from the Atlantic is forced into a narrow channel and rises in height by up to 50 ft (15 m). The speed of the water increases to an average of 10 mph (16 km/h). Dave Lawson holds the record for the longest river tidal wave to be ridden by a surfer—he traveled a distance of 5.7 mi (9.2 km) in 40 minutes.

A surfer rides the waves on the River Severn bore.

MONSTER WAVE
The highest wave at sea verified in modern times was a 280-ft (85-m) wave that struck Japan's Ryukyu Islands in 1771. The wave was powerful enough to toss a huge rock, weighing over 75 tons, more than 1 mi (1.6 km) inland.

Deep Blue Sea The deepest point in the ocean bed is 1.25 times deeper than Mount Everest is tall! A staggering depth of 35,830 ft (10,921 m) has been recorded in the Marianas Trench in the Pacific Ocean.

Delving the Depths On January 23, 1960, the U.S. Navy bathysphere *Trieste* descended to a depth of 35,797 ft (10,911 m), the deepest point descended to in the Marianas Trench.

Clear as Glass The water of the Weddell sea off Antarctica is so clear that you can see small objects more than 260 ft (79 m) below the surface!

Undersea Jet The water coming from one underwater hot spring, 300 mi (483 km) off the U.S. West Coast, is 759°F (404°C).

Freshwater Ocean Freshwater from the mouth of the Amazon River extends between 100 and 160 mi (160 and 255 km) into the Atlantic ocean.

Bed of Mud Beyond the mouth of the Amazon River are deep deposits of mud and other sediments carried by the river. These deposits form a cone that is 425 mi (685 km) long and 160 mi (260 km) wide. The mud is 36,000 ft (11,000 m) deep, more than 6,000 ft (1,829 m) deeper than Mount Everest is high!

An island in a lake on an island in a lake on an island! The surface of the lake in Taal Volcano on the Philippine Islands is below sea level.

Pacific Jacuzzi Geologists have estimated that there might be as many as one million volcanoes on the floor of the Pacific Ocean. So far, more than 5,000 active sub-marine volcanoes have been discovered.

Mighty Amazon The amount of fresh water pouring from the mouth of the Amazon into the Atlantic Ocean in one day would be enough to satisfy the entire water needs of the U.S. for five months.

Flight from the Deep The deepest underwater escape was made by Roger Chapman and Roger Mallinson from a depth of 1,575 ft (480 m) off the coast of Ireland in 1973. Their vessel, *Pisces III*, had sunk and they remained trapped for 76 hours before escaping.

The highest waves regularly ridden by surfers are at Waimea Bay, Hawaii. The waves at this bay frequently rise to a staggering 30–35 ft (9–11 m).

High Deposits On the Hawaiian island of Lane there are sediments that were deposited by waves at a height of more than 1,200 ft (366 m) above the sea. Such huge waves could only be caused by a massive landfall underwater.

Tsunami Rider The greatest wave ever ridden by a surfer was a wall of water about 50 ft (15 m) high. It was probably a tsunami (a wave created by an earthquake). It was ridden in 1868 on the ocean off the Hawaiian island of Minole by a Hawaiian surfer who was caught by the wave.

Underwater Everest The tallest underwater mountain is nearly as tall as Mount Everest. A seamount between Samoa and New Zealand rises 28,500 ft (8,687 m).

Towering Wave A U.S. serviceman on board the USS *Ramapo* in the Pacific in 1933 recorded a wave 112 ft (34 m) high. This wave was nearly twice as high as the bust of Abraham Lincoln on Mount Rushmore.

Seabed and Breakfast A hotel beneath the waves is under construction off the coast of Dubai, in the United Arab Emirates. Access will be through a glass tube from the reception area onshore.

Running Water The strongest ocean current is the Antarctic Circumpolar Drift that flows at nearly 7 billion cu ft (2 billion cu m) per second in the confined passage between South America and Antarctica.

"A wave twice as high as the bust of Lincoln on Mount Rushmore"

Deep Salvage In 1992 a wreck 17,250 ft (5,258 m) below the waves was salvaged by the USS *Salvor*.

Room at the Bottom Richard Presley spent 69 days underwater in a module at Key Largo, Florida, in 1992.

Wandering Raft A raft called the *La Balta* drifted 8,600 mi (13,840 km) across the Pacific Ocean from Ecuador to Australia in 1973.

Six Months Adrift Maurice and Maralyn Bailey were adrift on a raft in the Pacific Ocean for 177 days after a whale sank their boat.

Surviving Alone Poon Lim, a British seaman, was adrift 133 days alone on a raft in 1943.

The Strokkur hot spring geyser in Iceland sends jets of boiling water and hot steam 115 ft (35 m) into the air every seven to ten minutes. Iceland has more than 700 geysers and hot springs.

European Record The hot water springs at Polichnitos, on the Greek island of Lesvos, are the hottest in Europe. The water bubbles from the ground at temperatures of between 169°F and 196°F (76°C and 91°C).

Snow Bathing Iceland's natural hot water feeds the Blue Lagoon, a pool whose waters look frosty blue. The water, however, averages 104°F (40°C) and its mineral-rich properties have medical powers. In winter, bathers enjoy the hot water while temperatures are way below zero and the pool is surrounded by snow.

Himalayan Heat Water gushes from the hot springs of Manikaran, in the Indian Himalayan foothills, at 201°F (94°C) for those able to stand the high temperature. Regular dips in the Manikaran spring—the world's hottest—are said to cure all kinds of skin diseases. Rice will cook in Manikaran spring water in 20 minutes.

ICELANDIC BANANAS

Hot water springs feed pipes that heat the buildings of the Iceland's capital, Reyjavik. Hot water pipes are also used to heat greenhouses that grow fruit and vegetables that could not survive in the open. A bunch of bananas grown in an Icelandic greenhouse heated in this way was once presented to British prime minister, Sir Winston Churchill.

Hot Water Much of the water in Norris Geyser Basin in America's Yellowstone National Park is hotter than the boiling point. A scientific drill digging at nearly 1,000 ft (325 m) below the surface measured a temperature of 459°F (237°C). Yellowstone contains more than 10,000 thermal features, including about 500 geysers—more than 60 percent of the world's geysers.

Tallest Geyser The tallest geyser in the world is Steamboat geyser, in Yellowstone National Park. The geyser throws water between 300 and 400 ft (100 and 135 m) in the air during eruptions. The problem for visitors is that it is temperamental. Its highest eruption was in the 1950s and Steamboat has not thrown a really high water spout since May 2000.

Roaring Tide

In a matter of hours, Canada's Bay of Fundy daily fills with water as high as a four-story building. Twice a day, the world's highest tides create a difference of between 24 and 54 ft (7 and 16 m) in the depth of the seawater—the average difference is 48 ft (14 m). At mid-tide, the currents in the bay give out a roar that is known locally as "the voice of the moon."

The low tide exposes a "flowerpot" rock in the Bay of Fundy, on which a lone tree grows.

Regular as Clockwork Yellowstone National Park's Old Faithful Geyser gets its name because of the regularity of its eruptions. It erupts every 63 to 75 minutes. Nearby Anemone Geyser is even more predictable: it erupts every seven to ten minutes. Anemone's pools fill with water that splashes as it boils. When the water is thrown up 10 ft (3 m) in to the air, the pool drains completely.

Acidity Echinus Geyser in Yellowstone National Park is the highest acid-water geyser in the world. It erupts to a height of 40 to 60 ft (12 to 18 m).

In Hot Water Thermopolis, Wyoming, boasts the world's largest hot water spring. The first written account of the spring, in 1776, recorded that a rattlesnake had fallen in the hot water and been cooked. The main spring at Thermopolis gushes 18,600,00 gal (84,500 million l) of water a day.

"Chess pieces in hot water"

Chess boards and pieces are provided for bathers who dip into the hot springs in Budapest, Hungary!

Index

Index

ACKNOWLEDGMENTS

Jacket (t/l) Ripley's Entertainment Inc; (b/l) Dragon News/Rex Features; (b/r) Alex Sudea/Rex Features; (t/r) Rex Features

6 (b) Ciro Fusco/AFP/GETTYIMAGE; 7 (l) NASA/AFP/GETTYIMAGE; 8 (t) William West/AFP/GETTYIMAGE, (b) William West/AFP/GETTYIMAGE; 9 (t) Lloyd Cluff/CORBIS; 10 (b) IBL/REX; 11 (t) Alex Sudea/REX; 12 (t) Sipa Press/REX, (b) Miura Dolphins/AFP/GETTYIMAGE; 13 (t) David Hill/REX; 14 (b) Davis Factor/CORBIS; 15 (b/r) DiMaggio/Kalish/CORBIS; 16 (t) Roy Garner/REX, (b/l) AFP/GETTYIMAGE; 17 (t) Tom Bean/CORBIS; 18 (t) Jens Buettner/AFP/GETTYIMAGE; 20 (l) Bettmann/CORBIS, (r) Bettmann/CORBIS; 21 (b) Sunday Time/CORBIS SYGMA; 22 (b) Dragon/REX; 23 (b) Victor Vasenin/AFP/GETTYIMAGE; 24 (t) PIERRE VERDY/AFP/GETTYIMAGE; 25 (t) JAC/REX; 26 (b) Sipa Press /REX; 27 (r) AFP/GETTYIMAGE; 28 (t) Christopher Gerigk/AFP/GETTYIMAGE, (c/r) Gred Garay/AFP/GETTYIMAGE, (b) Kevin Schafer/CORBIS; 29 (b) Philippe Hays/REX; 30 (r) Simon Walker/REX; 31 (b) Rick Doyle/CORBIS; 32 (b) Richard Sowersby/REX; 33 (t) Paul A. Souders/CORBIS, (b) Patrick Barth/REX

All other photos are from Corel, PhotoDisc, Digital Vision and Ripley's Entertainment Inc.